1

THE ORIGIN OF THE NAME OF GOD AND HIS TRUE IDENTITY

Synopsis and Translation of the Phoenician, Ugaritic, Canaanite, Sumerian, Akkadian, and Assyrian Tablets.

Excerpts from

Are we worshiping a fake god?

How Babylonian and Phoenician Gods Became Yahweh and the god of Christians!

First Edition, published in 1963, in French, in France.
Second Edition, published in 2008, in English, under the title "Anunnaki Greatest Secrets Revealed by the Phoenicians and Ulema: Are we worshiping a fake God?" in the United States, ISBN: 978-1-312-37654-0.
Third Edition, published in 2013, in the United States, in two formats: a) Paperback, b)Amazon Kindle Edition.

***   ***   ***

Date of Publication: July 23, 2014
Published by Times Square Press, WJNA, Inc., New York and Berlin.

Website of the author:
www.maximilliendelafayettebibliography.org/biblio
Contact: Marla Cohen at newyorkgate@aol.com

Maximillien de Lafayette

THE ORIGIN OF THE NAME OF GOD AND HIS TRUE IDENTITY

Synopsis and Translation of the Phoenician, Ugaritic, Canaanite, Sumerian, Akkadian, and Assyrian Tablets.

THE ORIGIN OF THE NAME OF GOD AND HIS TRUE IDENTITY

Synopsis and Translation of the Phoenician, Ugaritic, Canaanite, Sumerian, Akkadian, and Assyrian Tablets.

Maximillien de Lafayette

*** *** ***

Times Square Press
New York Berlin Paris Madrid
2014

Table Of Contents

- Prologue
- The real name of God.
- Allah's terminology.
- Yahweh was a common Phoenician name.
- The Phoenician source.
- The Phoenician words "Yehaw", "Yehi", "Yaw", and "Yeuo" are the origin of the Hebrew words "Yah", "Yahu", and "Yahweh".
- Israelites bore the name of the Phoenician god Baal.
- Appearances of the word Yahweh outside and before the Bible was written (To name a few).
- The origins of Yahwehism.
- Phoenicia was the original source for the Hebrew Yahweh's imagery in the Bible and the "Cherubim Throne".
- Yahweh-Elohim and the Phoenician-Ugaritic Bull-Gods and the golden calves.
- Yahweh, and Ea/Enki create a spring in the Garden of Eden.
- Yahweh fighting the Dragon.
- "The Most High" epithet.
- On Monotheism.
- Epilogue: Quotes from leading scholars, authors, Sumeriologists and Assyriologists.

*** *** ***

Prologue

The name of God "Yahweh", his attributes and extraordinary (Supernatural) powers and deeds were borrowed from pagans' gods; gods the Israelites worshiped before they "created" their own god "Yahweh", who centuries later, became the God of the Christians and the Muslims.

So is it fair and logical to assume that we are worshiping a "Pagans' God" or more precisely an amalgam of mythical gods? You bet!

And this is exactly, the delicate, fragile and controversial topic we will be exploring, discussing and explaining in this treatise. If you are fanatically religious and you believe every word in the Bible, and all the stories rabbis, sheiks, Imams, bishops and priests tell you, then, do not read this treatise, because it could disturb you, and lead you to believe that it was written to discredit your faith and your beliefs in the Jewish Bible, the Torah, Talmud, the Christian Bible (New Testament), Jesus, the Christian Church, the Koran, and the Prophets.

And this is not the case at all.

It is not my intention to dishonor your religion or ridicule whatever you believe in. Never, ever!

Before you read any part of this treatise, I want to inform you that this publication does not attack any religion. Far from it.

My conclusions are based upon linguistic, historical, geographical, and archaeological facts and irrefutable findings, scrolls and inscriptions written centuries before any organized religion was established on Earth, and the word "GOD" was ever pronounced by or known to mankind.

11

Those who claim that God, his names and role is a matter of semantics are wrong. It is neither a semantic nor a linguistic matter at all. It is not the name per se, nor the language that defines the nature of God and proves his existence, and by the way why not *her* existence?

Who can explain to me and who can prove to me that God is indeed Masculine and not Feminine?

The enormous differences in defining "God" arise when we attempt to explain his origin and nature in English, in French, in Greek, in Latin, in Arabic, or in any other language, according to the teachings, revelations and conceptions of various religious figures such as Abraham, Tut-ankh-amoun, Melkart, Moses, Elijah, Noah, Enoch, Jesus, Mohammad, Moses and New Age gurus.

So, it is not a matter of differences in names, or how God is written, pronounced, and spelled in different languages, but:

a-His true origin.

b-Where did he come from?

c-What is his real name?

d-How and why did Abraham, Moses, early believers, tribes, scribes, prophets, and others unintentionally or willingly change and/or misinterpret God's name or names?

e-How many names God had at the time, Abraham, Moses, and other prophets met him?

f-In what original language, his name was written?

What and how it was written?

And how it was translated in Greek, Latin, French, English, Spanish, etc.?

g-How did God himself pronounce his name?

h-Who heard God first?

i-When and where did the term or word "God" appear the first time in the history of humanity?

And what did it mean at that time; the very first time it was pronounced, used, and later put in writing?

Did the meaning change?

No?

Yes?

Why?

j-Any relation to the Anunnaki, the Ancient Gods, the Sumerians, the Phoenicians, the extraterrestrials?

Those are the vital and most important questions we must address and answer, not how to write God in Aramaic, Hebrew, Latin and English!

A major problem arises when some religions attach very particular "specifications" and attributes to their national gods. For instance, the Arabic word "Kabir" (Also in Turkish, Urdu, Persian, etc.) means great, big, majestic.

And the Arabic word "Akbar" means the greatest, the biggest, the superior. Now, we all know that Muslims call their god: Allah (Allahou) Akbar, meaning: Allah is the greatest, the biggest, the superior.

And here is the problem according to Jewish scholars; why did the Muslims call their God, "The Superior and the Greatest"?

What did the Muslims mean?

Is their Allah (God) greater than whom?

Superior to whom?

Bigger and superior to another god or other gods?

Certainly, the Muslims meant that Allah, their God is superior to the God of the Jews and the Christians, explained Jewish scholars and theologians.

It is very bizarre indeed, because the Jews themselves think the same thing about their own God (Yahweh). According to the Jewish tradition, Yahweh is the Only God, the True God, above all other gods!

In Exodus 20:2-17, and Deuteronomy 5:6-21, we read what God has said to Moses: "I am the Lord your God, who brought you out of the land of Egypt, out of the house of

13

slavery…Do not have any other gods before me…You shall not bow down to them or worship them; for I the Lord your God am a jealous God, punishing children for the iniquity of parents, to the third and the fourth generation of those who reject me…"

But God Enki/Ea (The Anunnaki God)) said the same thing to Abraham or AV-raham (Another historical and controversial Abraham). Enki said to Abraham that he is the only god, the superior god, the greatest god…the greatest of all of them.

It seems to me that the Gods are competing against each other. Now, if you do not believe that the Anunnaki Enki/Ea was in fact Yahweh, no problem, remove Enki from the picture, get rid of this comparison or reference, and read the Sumerian texts instead.

You will find EXACTLY the same words, the same phrases, the same divine description and threats; the same speech Enki/Ea gave in the Sumerian epics! Enki/Ea spoke to Abraham, in the same manner, Yahweh spoke to Moses, in the same way, Allah spoke to Mohammed, in the same way, God spoke to the early saints, bishops and doctors of the Christian Church!

Apparently, even today, God is still speaking in the same manner to our flamboyant televangelists and broadcasting preachers who drive Porsche and Mercedes.

Jesus said the same thing! In the first edition of the Aramaic/Syriac-Arabic Biblical text, we read Jesus saying: "Ana Nour Al Alam…Wal Hak", meaning:" I am the Light of the Universe…and the Truth", and later on, the Church theologians crafted the Holy Trinity concept, and Jesus became the real God of the World; God The Creator, Jesus the son of God, and "one" with the Holy Spirit. All are ONE, three in one, indivisible, and the same! This is the kind of thought and prolific literature we get from organized religions!

The objectives and purposes of this treatise are to explore, understand, and reveal the true origin and nature of "God" as we know Him and revere Him today.

***   ***   ***

The real name of God.
Allah's terminology.
Yahweh was a common Phoenician name.

86% of Americans think that "Allah" is the god of the Muslims, and "Allah" is not the god of the Christians; the Judeo-Christian God, that is.

Those 86% are 100% wrong!! "Allah" is an Arabic word; a term meaning the creator of the universe and mankind.

"Allah" also is a Christian word! Really?

Of course! Because the word "Allah" was used some 656 years before the Prophet Mohammad was born and before Islam came to life.

"Allah" is an Arabic word used by Arabs who were NOT Muslims, but Christians who lived in the Arab world, in the Arab Peninsula, in North Africa, in the Near East, and in the Middle East, long longtime before Arabs were converted to Islam, and years and years and years before the birth of Mohammad, and the establishment of the Islamic religion.

The word "Allah" was used by the Eastern Christian priests, monks, hermits, and in the Christian mass of the Lebanese Maronites, the Egyptian Copts, the Syrian and Iraqi Syriac and Asshurian, the Roum, the Catholic literature and liturgy. Even today, and as we speak, all Christian Arabs (To name a few:

Maronites, Orthodox, Roum, Syriac, Copts, Assyrians, Armenians-Assyrians, Lebanese Armenian Syriac, and additional 13 different Christian denominations) have used and still use "Allah" as the one and only word for God.

So, "Allah" is a Christian Arabic word adopted by the Prophet Mohammad, the Koran, the Islamic religion, and the Muslims worldwide. However, Allah as a term, as a personage (creator of the universe), and as a Christian word for the creator of the universe and maker of the human race was not created by the early Christian Arabs either; they took it from the Aramaic word "Allah", and from the Phoenician "El", "Baal-El".

And so did the Hebrews and so many other civilizations and religions throughout the centuries. The Jewish-Hebrew-Judaic-Israelite Jehovah-Yahweh (Yahweh-Elohim) was the Phoenician god "El", "El-Baal", "Baal Hadad", also called Yaw, Yehaw, and Yehi in Phoenician…and also was the Anunnaki-Sumerian god "El-Enki or Ea".

The Phoenician "El" became "Eli" in Aramaic. And Jesus on the cross before relinquishing his last breath, called his heavenly father "Eli".

On the cross, Jesus said: "Eloi, Eloi, lamma sabachthani", or "Eloi, Eloi, lema sabachthani"; Matthew: "Eli, Eli, lama sabachthani", that is to say, "My God, my God, why hast thou forsaken me?" (xxvii, 46). Mark: "Eloi, Eloi, lama sabachthani", which is being interpreted, "My God, my God, why hast thou forsaken me?" (xv, 34.) The Hebrews too, used the Phoenician word "EL" as "Eli".

The plural of Eli (In Aramaic and Hebrew) is Elohim (My Gods, my Lords, and my Masters). The Arabs obliged, and the Christian and Muslim Arabs transformed "El" into: Elahi, Ilahi, Allah.

All came from the same ancient origin/source: Phoenician, and later, Aramaic. Historians, theologians and linguists agree. But what many priests, preachers, rabbis and sheiks are hiding from you – and most probably misleading you - is the origin, the primordial name and nature of the true God who became the god of their religion, and who replaced "El", the first god, early humans came to know, meet, discover, fear and obey!

18

The Phoenician source.

While it was/is forbidden to pronounce the name of Yahweh in Judaism -and at least out of religious courtesy in modern Jewish tradition- Yahweh was a common name in Phoenicia, and especially in Byblos, Batroun, Sidon, Ras Shamra, Nakoura, Tyre, and Ugarit. And it was written and pronounced in various ways, such as:

a- Yehi,
b- Yehaw,
c- Yehar,
d- Yah,
e- Yehu.

Many Phoenician males were called Yahweh-this, or Yahweh-that. And a few Phoenician kings used Yahweh as part of their first names, such as:

a- Yehaw-milk,
b- Yehar-baal.

For instance, in 1929, a 10th century B.C. inscription on an ancient Phoenician building built by Yehimilk, king of Byblos was found and contained the following: "May the assembly of the gods of Byblos, the king of Byblos, and Baal-shamem prolong the life of Yehi-milk…"

On another fragment of the tablet (Or slab), a passage reads as follows: "I am Yehaw-milk, the king of Byblos, the son of Yeh-ar-baal…"

Note: The name Yehi-milk is a very old word composed of two parts: a-Yehi, b-Milk, which means king.

From the Phoenician word "Milk", derived the Arabic and Hebrew word Malik/Malak, which also means king.

19

Not to confuse Malak with Malaak, which means angel in Hebrew, Aramaic and Arabic. Worth mentioning here that the words/names Yaw, Yeuo and Yaw, which gave birth to the word/name Yahweh were also found on an ancient Phoenician coin in Gaza, made during the Persian Period.

The coin had a Phoenician inscription and the image of the Phoenician sea god, then, called Yaw. Numerous historians and archaeologists have argued that the image on the Phoenician coin is indeed the image of the Hebrew Yahweh. Additional findings revealed that the word Yahweh was used and pronounced differently by the Phoenicians throughout the centuries. For instance, Yehi-milk was frequently used in the 10th century B.C., while Yehaw-milk was used in the 5th and the 4th centuries B.C., in various regions of Phoenicia and Syria (The Canaanite Land).

Numerous Sumerologists and Assyriologists believe that Yah (Referring to Yahweh) originated from the Assyro-Babylonian word "Ya'u", which was the name of an Assyrian-Babylonian god, and later in history, the words "Ya'u" and "Yah" were written as "Jah" in Mesopotamian epics, poems, and myths.

While a greater number of linguists and historians argued that "Ya'u" was an alternative name and a Mesopotamian pronunciation of the Phoenician word "Yau" and/or "Wau".

The Jewish Bible (Old Testament) confirmed that Yahweh was called Baal (Name of a Phoenician god) by some Israelites. From Hosea 2:16: "And in that day, says the Lord, you will call me, 'My Husband,' and no longer will you call me, 'My Ba'al.' For I will remove the names of the Ba'als from her mouth, and they shall be mentioned by name no more."

In conclusion, Yahweh-Elohim, the God of Israel who became the god of the Christians and Muslims, absorbed the names, attributes, descriptions, epithets, and the glorious feats of the gods of Mesopotamia and Canaan, who were his rivals, and became the subject and theme of Israel's prophets hysterical attacks on Phoenicia and Ugarit's gods.

The history of ancient religions of the Middle East and the Near East revealed that Yahweh-Elohim was a colorful amalgam of earlier pagans' gods, centuries before the Jewish Bible was written. The Israelite Yahweh is de facto, a recast/replica of Yaw, Bel, Baal of the Phoenician-Ugartic myths, and other Anunnaki gods.

Yahweh was already a holy name used in Canaanite literature, centuries before the Mosaic epoch.

Yahweh is a combination of the traits and attributes of Yaw/Yam/Baal of the Phoenician-Ugaritic Myths (1500-1200 B.C.) and Babylon's Anuna, thousands of years before the Hebraic monotheistic religion was established.

The Hebraic scribes and writers of the Old Testament fused the Ugaritic El (Bull-El), Yaw and Baal together into the new image of Yahweh-Elohim of the Jewish Bible.

*** *** ***

The Phoenician words "Yehaw", "Yehi", "Yaw", and "Yeuo" are the origin of the Hebrew words "Yah", "Yahu", and "Yahweh".

The Phoenician name Yehaw-milk, which was also used as Yehi, Yehaw, and Yehar which meant "Yehaw is king", as well as the name of the Phoenician/Canaanite sea-god Yaw or Yeuo gave birth to the Hebrew words Yah, Yahweh and Yahu.

The image of Yaw/Yeuo which was found on a ancient coin from Gaza, made during the Persian period of Greek artifact and craftsmanship, was in fact, the first historical image of the Hebrew God, Yahweh; a god, the Phoenicians worshipped under the name of Yehi-milk (10th century B.C.) and Yehaw-milk (5th/4th century B.C.)

As soon as the Israelites destroyed the Canaanites (Syrians and Phoenicians), they ascribed all the mighty and supernatural attributes, powers, and glory of the Canaanite and Mesopotamian gods to their own and newly created "GOD" Yahweh.

And Yahweh became the one and only true god, not Baal, El, or Bel. And afterward, Christianity and Islam used the same scenario. To the Christians, Jesus became God.

And to the Muslims, Allah became the one and only god, not Jesus, Yaw, Yahweh, Baal or Bel.

The absolute truth is that the newly created Hebrew god "Yahweh" is *de facto*, an amalgam of the Mesopotamian, Egyptian, Hittite, and Canaanite (Syrian and Phoenician) gods and goddesses. Linguists, theologians and historians of religions, easily recognized the new divine persona and attributes given to Yahweh by the Hebrews, simply by comparing the new Hebrew's attributions to their god, with the old epithets and attributes of gods Baal Saphon (Baal Hadad), El, Seth, Sopdu, Shamash, Tammuz, Anu, Enki, and Enlil.

If you compare the epithets and attributes of the Anunnaki god Marduck with those of Yahweh and Allah, you will find out that they are almost identical.

Marduck had 50 to 90 titles.

Allah has "99 Asma' Al Lah Al-Housna", which means the 99 noble names of Allah, and Yahweh is no exception.

*** *** ***

Israelites bore the name of the Phoenician god Baal.

It is a fact that a considerable number of the early Israelites bore the name of God Baal, as did and still do, people from neighboring countries, and even in Latin America, through out the centuries.

Millions of Muslims have as a first name "Mohammad", which is the name of the Prophet Mohammad. In Latin America, the tradition continues to the present day; there are hundreds of thousands of men who are called Jesus.

So, it is not unconceivable that some Israelites bore the name of Phoenician deities such as Baal. Sons of Saul, the first king of Israel were called Baal.

And as told by Hosea, Yahweh was also called Baal. But the trend of naming Israelites Baal ceased when Israel waged a war against the Ugaritic and Phoenicians when the Hebrew prophets and scribes began to feel the direct threat of the Phoenician religion to their Judaism and Hebraic religion, between 1200 and 587 B.C.

*** *** ***

Appearances of the word Yahweh outside and before the Bible was written (To name a few).

The word Yahweh and its divine elements were found:

1-In inscriptions on Ramesses III's temple in Medinet Habu, which contained the words Yah-wa and Yi-ha, which scholars and linguists have associated these 2 Syrian words with the Hebrew word Yah-weh, circa 1400 B.C.

2-On the list of Rameses II, which was discovered in an ancient Nubian temple in Amara (Amarah). Number of listing: 93-98.

3-In the Canaanite inscription "Yah of Gat" on an ewer from the late Bronze Age, which was found in the ruins of a temple at Lachish.

4-On the "Stele of Mesh'a", Anet 320 (9th century).

5-An archaeological excavation which revealed the names of Aramean princes from the 8th B.C., which contained the element Yau, and which was occasionally pronounced Yah.
6-In an ostracon from Kuntillet Ajrud 246, from the 8th century.

7-In the Egyptian list of names of places, which was discovered in Amon temple of Amenhotep III, located in Soleb in Nubia.

8-In the Adad and Lachish letters, Anet, 569, 322, from the 6th century.

9-In the Murashu archives from the reign of Artaxerxes and Darius, discovered at Nippur, and which contained the word

Ja-a-ma (Jawa), which is associated with the divine element of Yahweh.

10-In an ancient Egyptian clay tablet referring to Ahi-Jami, the mayor of Ta'anach in Canaan. Ahi-Jami was also pronounced and written as Ahi-ja and Ahi-Yah; two names closely related to the divine status of Yahweh, at the time it was referred to and written as Ja-mi (Yah-mi). Said tablet can be found in the archives of the Museum of Cairo.

11-In an archeological find referring to Sa-rar (Also known as Seir in Edom) which historians and archaeologists have associated Yahweh with Seir and Paran.

12-In the lists of Egyptian names which contained the name and location of an ancient site in Syria, called Yah-wa, Number's reference 97.

13-Three Amorite tablets displayed at the British Museum in 1908, which contained "Yaum-ilu", "Ya'we-ilu", and "Yawe-ilu", referring to the three ancient forms of the primordial name of Yahweh as 'Jahweh is God". Worth noting here that "Yah", corresponds to the Biblical "Jah" of Psalm 114:35. There is no doubt that the first component of "Ya'wa-ilu" is the name of Yahweh.

14-In the list of names at Mari, from the second millennium B.C., and Yahweh appeared as an Amorite name under Yahwi.

15-In Assyrian records: In the annals of Tiglathpileser III which included the name of Azri-Yau, who was a Syrian king. We should keep in mind that Yahweh was worshiped in Syria and Phoenicia and not just in Israel. And it was customary for Canaanite kings to have Yahwehistic names, especially in the first millennium B.C.

Yahwehistic names also appeared during the reign of Sargon II. In fact, numerous Assyrian texts and records included those names and their elements. One of those names mentioned in the Assyrian records was Yau-bidi, a ruler of Hamath.

16-In the Mari archives from the second millennium B.C. (circa 18th century B.C.) which contained names of Amorites known to be Yahweh's names, such as: Yawiya, Yawidim, Yawium, Yawiila, Yawid, Yausib, and Yawi. Worth mentioning here, the derivation and relation of Yahweh, Yausib, Yaahwi and Yaahwi, and their causative verbal forms.

Yaah-wi derived from the Ugaritic and Phoenician word "hwy", which also appeared as "hyw" in Ethiopian, and as "hyy" in Arabic, Aramaic and Hebrew, and meant "be, to be, to become, and to give life."
However, if could also mean "to appear, to be present, and to manifest" taken into consideration the definition and meaning of the word "yahwi" (yaahwi) in Amorite.
The two similar sentences in Amorite and archaic Phoenician-Proto Ugaritic "Yaahwi ilum" and "Yahwi ilu" mean the god who manifests himself. The word "ilu" and related elements were concurrently used as "el", "il", "eli", "Ilum" (Akkadian), in Phoenician, Ugaritic, Hebrew and even Arabic, since the Arabic words "Ilahi" (My god), "Ilah" (God) and "Alaah" were used in ancient and modern Arabic. Yawi (Ya-wi) is obviously a variant of "Yaah-wi (Ya-ah-wi). Grosso modo, it is epistemologically based upon "hwy", which is associated with the Akkadian "ewu", the Aramaic "hwh" and "hwy".

17-In the letter sent by Iawa-ila "Iawi-Ilâ", the Syrian king of Tal-hayum to Zimri-lim king of Mari (circa1782-1759 B.C.) Note: The element "iawi" of the Amorite names and

26

the Hebrew god's name originated from the same root, and was considered a divine name in both Hebrew and Amorite languages.

The Amorite names "Iawi-Ila", "Iawi Abdu", "Iahwi-Nasi", and "Iwahi-Sibu" also appeared in the "Mari Archives". God Nasi is a form of the word "Malik" (King). The word or term "Nasi" in archaic Hebrew is closely associated with "Elohim" (God/Gods).

Numerous Orientalists, Assyriologists and Sumerologists have suggested that Yahweh should be rendered ya'wa.

18-On the 10th century B.C. inscription on an ancient Phoenician building built by Yehimilk (Yehi-milk), king of Byblos, which was discovered in 1929.

19-In late old Babylonian Texts (circa 1800-1600 B.C.) where several Amorite personal names were mentioned with a "yawi" element, such as Yawium, the King of Kish (Modern day Tall al-Uhaymir), a contemporary of Abraham who lived nearby.

Numerous scholars, Assyriologists and linguists agreed that the form "yawi" of Mari Archives (circa 1800-1700 B.C) and "Yawium" of Kish (circa 1800-1600 B.C.) among other texts from Ur and Babylon which clearly mentioned all the elements and epistemological derivations of Yah-weh, retrace the origin of the Hebrew word/name Yahweh and Yahwehism.

And since Abraham who lived around 1800-1600 B.C. in that part of the world, it is logical to conclude that he learned about a god called Yahweh, and about "Yawi" and consequently borrowed the names and added his Biblical twist upon.

***   ***   ***

The origins of Yahwehism.

The origins of Yahwehism are not found in the Sinai Desert-Negeb as falsely claimed by the scribes of the Old Testament.

It is proven by archaeology, forensic anthropology, and philology that Yahwehism originated in, and from the Phoenician cities of Ugarit and Mari in Syria, and Ur of the Chaldees/Sumer.

The Israelites/Hebrews admitted that their ancestors were Arameans/Syrians. Deuteronomy 26:5 "And thou shalt speak and say before the Lord thy God: 'A Syrian ready to perish was my father; and he went down into Egypt and sojourned there with a few, and became there a nation, great, mighty, and populous." Other translation: Deuteronomy 26:5 (CEB "Common English Bible"): "Then you should solemnly state before the Lord your God: My father was a starving Aramean. He went down to Egypt, living as an immigrant there with few family members, but that is where he became a great nation, mighty and numerous."

In the Pentateuch, the Hebrew scribes fused two separate and totally different stories and historical origins of two periods:
a-The Bronze Age Canaanite.
b-The Iron Age Aramean.

In 560 B.C., the Hebrew scribes who wrote the story of the Exodus (2 Kings 25:27) were totally ignorant of the fact that their "Newly named and discovered" Yahweh, existed already under similar or quasi-similar names in much older scriptures, texts and stories from the Bronze Age, and Yahweh's attributes were taken from the attributes and epithets of the gods of Ugarit, Mari, Sumer, Egypt and other regions of Canaan, such as Enki of Mesopotamia, Baal-

Zephon of the Hyksos, Baal-Hadad, and Bel of Ugarit, Tyre, Sidon and Byblos, and Seth of Egypt.

"The Anunnaki god, Enki survived, if at all, in new guises, under different names...If Enki and his city-state had all but disappeared, literary traditions and religious syncretism kept something of them alive.

The two traditions that formed the basis of Western civilization, Greek and Biblical, appear to know stories of Enki, in much disguised form. In one sense we are very much the inheritors of civilization in its early, Sumerian forms; but in another sense we will always have a difficult time recognizing such early debts."-From "Traces of the Fugitive God. p.154", and "Myths of Enki, the Crafty God" by Samuel Noah Kramer and John Maier. Oxford University Press. 1989.

*** *** ***

Phoenicia was the original source for the Hebrew Yahweh's imagery in the Bible and the "Cherubim Throne".

The Phoenician gods seated on the winged sphinx thrones of Byblos (Identical to the Anunnaki-Sumerian thrones) were the prototypes of Yahweh's Cherubim throne in the Temple of Jerusalem.

The Hebrews transmuted the sphinx into angels (Cherubim). As a matter of fact, the early Hebrew Cherubim were depicted as humans with the heads of winged sphinxes.

One picture is worth a 1,000 words.

Hebrews worshipping the Anunnaki-Sumerian god Ea.
Abraham was one of the early Hebrews who worshipped Ea.
This was confirmed on numerous Sumerian, Assyrian, Akkadian, Babylonian,
Syrian and Phoenician tablets, seals and coins
found in Eridu, Ur of the Chaldees, Ugarit, Babylon,
and the Syrian town of Ebla.

According to 1 Sam 4:4, Yahweh, the God of Israel was "He who sitteth (on) the cherubim."
In addition, many Phoenician kings (Messengers of the Gods) were depicted as divine monarchs seated on a large stone or marble throne (Circa 1200-800 B.C.) supported on

each side by cherubim, and found in Megiddo, Byblos (Modern day Jbeil), Hamath and Tyre (Modern day Sour). The most famous throne belonged to King Hiram of Phoenicia seated on a cherub throne. Yahweh also sat on a cherub throne.

*** *** ***

Yahweh-Elohim and the Phoenician-Ugaritic Bull-Gods and the golden calves.

Short after the alleged apparition of Yahweh-Elohim to Moses at Mt. Sinai as a thundercloud, a Hebraic golden calf was fashioned in a Phoenician style. Apparently, there is a connection between the Phoenician "Calf" and the Israelites' reason for fashioning their own golden calf.

At that time in history, the Hebrew god was depicted as "Bull-Calf" in the image of the Phoenician, Ugaritic and Hyksos gods, Bull-El, and Baal-Hadad of the Bronze Age. The "Bull" image or at least the "Bull" symbol played a paramount role in the early Hebrew Scriptures and beliefs. This, became evident and unquestionable when the Hebrews used the Hyksos-Ugaritic Bull (Baal-Hadad) as symbol for their escape from Egypt.

*** *** ***

Yahweh, and Ea/Enki create a spring in the Garden of Eden:

From the Akkadian-Sumerian clay tablets we know that Ea "Enki" created a huge fountain (A pond, a lake, a river) in the garden of Idin (Eden). The Bible told us that Yahweh created a spring in the Garden of Eden (The same garden) which gave birth to four ancient rivers, called the Euphrates, the Hiddekel, the Pishon and the Gihon.

Numerous Mesopotamian slabs and seals depicted Ea "Enki" as an imposing god seated on a high throne with four or five streams of water (in the form of rivers) emanating from and/or around his shoulders. One of the characteristics and attribute of Ea is "The God of water", frequently

33

associated with "Apsu" which means in Sumero-Akkadian, ground-water.

Numerous Mesopotamian clay tablets depicted Ea "Enki" as a god inhabiting the "Apsu", and "Apsu" is where he dwells. As such, he is the universal creator, for water was needed to create the world. In the Koran, we find a reference made to Allah as the creator of the universe, because he created water.

The Koran stated, "Wa Khalakna Lakoum min Al Ma'I, Koula Chay'en Hay", which means verbatim, "And we have created for you from the water each life-form (Or each living creature).

In the old-Babylonian epics, water played a paramount and primordial role; water gave birth to the world, and water through the Great Deluge destroyed the world. Unforgettable historical figures in the Sumero-Akkadian epics were commonly and frequently associated with water, such as Pir-napishtim (Also called Utnapishtim, Ziusudra and Atrahasis) who became the Hebrew Noah.

In fact, the Hebrew story of the Great Deluge is the same story of the old Babylonian Deluge, which is *de facto*, the flood of the Mesopotamian Euphrates River.

*** *** ***

Yahweh fighting the Dragon.

The Mesopotamian clay tablets told us a story of God Marduk who fought and slaughtered Tiamat the dragon, in order to rule over the world.

In the Phoenician-Ugaritic story of "Baal Cycle", the Phoenician god Baal-Hadad fought the Lotan "Tannin" (dragon), the seven headed serpent-dragon of the sea located at a close proximity to Ugarit and Israel.

The Phoenician-Ugaritic dragon story was very well-known to the Hebrews who shared their borders with Phoenicia.

In the Jewish Bible, Yahweh fought the sea's dragon Leviathan.

Isaiah 27:1 "In that day Jehovah with his hard and great and strong sword will punish leviathan the swift serpent, and leviathan the crooked serpent; and he will slay the monster that is in the sea."

Psalm 74:12-14 "Yet God is my King of old, Working salvation in the midst of the earth. Thou didst divide the sea by thy strength: Thou brakest the heads of the sea-monsters in the waters. Thou brakest the heads of leviathan in pieces; Thou gavest him to be food to the people inhabiting the wilderness." The book of Job describes in detail Yahweh's fight and the fire of the dragon. Job 41: "Canst thou draw out leviathan with a fishhook? Or press down his tongue with a cord? Canst thou put a rope into his nose? Or pierce his jaw through with a hook? His sneezings flash forth light, And his eyes are like the eyelids of the morning. Out of his mouth go burning torches, And sparks of fire leap forth. Out of his nostrils a smoke goeth, As of a boiling pot and burning rushes. His breath kindleth coals, and a flame goeth forth from his mouth."

Unquestionably, the Biblical story of Yahweh fighting the dragon is copied from the "Baal Cycle", an Ugaritic story of god Baa-Hadad who fought against Yam. The 13th century B.C. myth (Story) of the Phoenician god Baal-Hadad told us that he fought his brother Yam, also called Nahar, to dominate Earth and to rule over the whole world, while the Jewish story was written in 586 B.C.

(Note: Some historians have claimed that the Biblical story was written between 588 and 1200 B.C.)

The Biblical story of the Hebrew God Yahweh fighting Baal-Hadad is simply a reproduction of chapter two of the Ugaritic myth of Yaw (Yahweh) fighting against Baal for the domination of Earth. And the Phoenician dragon mythical story resurfaced once again in the New Testament.

Revelation 13:1 "...and he stood upon the sand of the sea. And I saw a beast coming up out of the sea, having ten horns, and seven heads, and on his horns ten diadems, and upon his heads names of blasphemy."-100 CE.

Many of the early Israelites saw Yahweh as a subordinate to the Phoenician god El. And thus, they equated him with Baal, the Canaanite god they worshiped, and whose attributes were given to Yahweh. Yahweh was depicted as a storm-god who ruled over the waters. And Baal too, was a storm-god who conquered and dominated the waters, symbolized by a sea serpent and a sea-dragon.

The Psalms described Yahweh conquering and subduing the waters by destroying Rab and Leviathan the dragons, exactly as did the Phoenician God Baal who conquered the waters and destroyed the "Tanin", the sea-dragon.

Thus, it is obvious that the Story of Yahweh fighting the dragon originated from the Phoenician story of Baal fighting the dragon.

*** *** ***

36

"The Most High" epithet.

Yahweh took on the attributes and feats of Sumerian and Phoenician gods. Yahweh, assimilated the personas and feats of Mesopotamian gods before Yahwehism was born.

Anunnaki gods and Enki's motifs and attributes appeared in Genesis as Yahweh-Elohim's attributes.

And later on, Christianity and Islam ascribed the Babylonian Anunna and Enki's motifs and epithets to Christ and Allah.

Professor Kramer pointed out the "Bible's indebtedness to motifs found in Sumerian (Anunnaki's texts) literature of the 4th-3rd millenniums B.C. (Canaanite early Bronze Age)".

He noted that "Enki the "Crafty God" is alive and well today, his feats and epithets having been ascribed and assimilated to later gods."

Professor Cohn (Professor Emeritus, University of Sussex, England) stated: "Yahweh did not -any more than Baal or Marduk- remain subordinate to the supreme god. It was normal for a people to exalt its patron god to a position of unique dignity, setting him above all other gods.

This happened to Yahweh too: he came to be identified with El. A common epithet of El was Elyon, meaning "the Most High."

In the psalms, Yahweh is likewise called 'the Most High,' and his dominance is as absolute as El's."

He added "All in all, the Israelite world-view in the days of the monarchy had much in common with the world views of the Canaanites, the Mesopotamians, even the Egyptians."

Yahweh also took on the attributes of Phoenician wives and consorts. Athirat, wife of the Phoenician god El became Asherah of the Bible.

And finally…

On Monotheism:

37

We were told that Yahwehism (Judaism) was the first monotheistic religion; the religion of One Supreme God who created himself and everything in the universe.

Well, this is not true! In an Egyptian Hymn to the Sun-God, written circa 1,400 B.C., we read that the Sun-God is "The primordial Being, who himself made himself...the one and only God..."

It is very clear that we are reading here a declaration of monotheism. It is documented that monotheism was introduced into Egypt by Amenophis IV, who called God Aton the "only God, the one, supreme, and only God."

This was expressed in an Egyptian hymn in praise to God Aton.

The hymn was translated and published in "Breasted's Development of Religion and Thoughts in Ancient Egypt."

In section 65 of the hymn we read: "O Sole God, whose powers no others (Other gods) have (Possessed). In section 110, we read, "Thou alone shining in thy form as living Aton."

In section 120, we read, "There is no other that knoweth Thee." No doubt, the Egyptian Hymn deeply influenced Psalm 104. Refer to "The Treasury of Ancient Egypt" by Weigall, published in London in 1911. Yahwehism was not the product of divine revelations to Abraham and to Moses while he was wandering in the Sinai Desert, according to 1 Kings 6:1 (Circa 1446 B.C.)

Archaeological excavations proved beyond the shadow of a doubt, that there is no presence of a Late Bronze Age in the Sinai Desert and at Mount Sinai (Jabal Mousa).

And the fact that the Hebrews/Israelites' names at that period in time and long after the alleged Exodus kept the theophoric "Yaw", is a strong indication that they retained their polytheistic beliefs and worship of several gods, simply because polytheism was their original religious heritage and their primordial social-religious beliefs-system.

*** *** ***

EPILOGUE
Quotes from leading scholars, authors, Sumeriologists and Assyriologists.

Professors Graves and Patai (1963) on the Hebrews borrowing the epithets and achievements of the pagan gods and ascribing them to Yahweh: "The titles and attributes of many other Near Eastern deities were successively awarded to Yahweh Elohim...

Prophets and Psalmists were as careless about the pagan origins of the religious imagery they borrowed, as priests were about the adaptation of heathen sacrificial rites to God's service. The crucial question was: in whose honour these prophecies and hymns should now be sung, or these rites enacted? If in honour of Yahweh Elohim, not Anath, Baal or Tammuz, all was proper and pious." (p. 28. Robert Graves & Raphael Patai. Hebrew Myths: The Book of Genesis. New York. Greewich House. 1983 reprint of 1963, 1964 editions)

Professor Blenkinsopp (of Notre Dame University) on Atrahasis and Gilgamesh motifs in Genesis:"...just as Genesis 1-11 as a whole corresponds to the structure of the Atrahasis myth, so the Garden of Eden story has incorporated many of the themes of the great Gilgamesh poem." (pp. 65-6. "Human Origins, Genesis 1:1-11:26." Joseph Blenkinsopp. The Pentateuch, An Introduction to the First Five Books of the Bible. New York. Doubleday. 1992.)

Graves and Patai on Adam's "Fall" being a possible reworking of Enkidu and Adapa: "Some elements of the Fall of Man myth in Genesis are of great antiquity. The

41

Gilgamesh Epic describes Enkidu shunned by the wild creatures; the priestess covered his nakedness...
Another source of the Genesis "Fall of Man" is the Akkadian myth of Adapa...This myth supplies the theme of the Serpent's warning to Eve..." (pp. 78-79. "The Fall of Man." Robert Graves & Raphael Patai. Hebrew Myths: The Book of Genesis. New York. Greewich House. 1983 reprint of 1963, 1964 edition.)

Professor Batto (1992) on the Hebrews recasting of earlier Mesopotamian myths and motifs in the Hebrew Bible: "...I want to emphasize that this new mythmaking process is a *conscious,* reflected application of older myths and mythic elements to new situations. In so far as one admits the presence of myth in ancient Babylonian and Canaanite culture, then one must also admit the presence of myth in the Bible.
This book, then, is a series of case studies of mythmaking in ancient Israel, or to be more exact, in the biblical tradition." (pp. 13-14. "Introduction." Bernard F. Batto. Slaying the Dragon, Mythmaking in the Biblical Tradition. Louisville, Kentucky. Westminster-John Knox Press. 1992.)
"Now the Yahwist's primeval narrative is itself a marvelous example of mythmaking based upon prior Mesopotamian myths, notably Atrahasis and Gilgamesh. Interestingly, the reappropriation of mythic traditions and in-tertextual borrowing posited for biblical writers was already present within ancient Babylonia, and illustrates those biblical writers must be understood within the larger ancient Near Eastern literary and theological tradition."
(p. 14. "Introduction." Bernard F. Batto. Slaying the Dragon, Mythmaking in the Biblical Tradition. Louisville, Kentucky. Westminster-John Knox Press. 1992)

Professor Lambert: The authors of ancient cosmologies were essentially compilers. Their originality was expressed in new combinations of old themes, and in new twists to old ideas." (p.107. W.G. Lambert. "A New Look at the Babylonian Background of Genesis." [1965], in Richard S. Hess & David T. Tsumra, Editors. *I Studied Inscriptions From Before the Flood*. Winona Lake, Indiana, Eisenbrauns, 1994)

Pinches on Ea possibly being a prototype of the Hebrew God Yah (note: Pir-napishtim is now rendered Utnapishtim, he is the "Mesopotamian Noah"), and that the Flood was a flooding Euphrates river (Note: Microscopic inspection of the flood sediments at Shuruppak where the Flood-Hero lived at the time he was warned of the pending flood, revealed freshwater laid silts and clays, suggesting a river flood):
"Professor Hommel, the well-known Assyriologist and Professor of Semitic languages at Munich, suggests that this god Ya is another form of the name Ea..." (p. 59. Theophilus G. Pinches. The Old Testament in the Light of the Historical Records and Legends of Assyria and Babylonia. London. Society For Promoting Christian Knowledge. 1908)

Pir-napishtim was himself a worshipper of Ae, and on account of that circumstance, he is represented in the story as being under the special protection of that god...It has been more than once suggested, and Professor Hommel has stated the matter as his opinion, that the name of the god Ae or Ea, another possible reading of which is Aa, may be in some way connected with, and perhaps originated the Assyro-Babylonian divine name Ya'u "god," which is cognate with the Hebrew Yah or, as it is generally written, Jah...There is one thing that is certain, and that is, that the Chaldean Noah, Pir-napishtim, was faithful in the worship of the older god, who therefore warned him, saving his life." (pp.112-114. "The Flood."

43

Theophilus G. Pinches. The Old Testament in the Light of the Historical Records and Legends of Assyria and Babylonia. London. Society For Promoting Christian Knowledge. 1908)

Kramer on "when" Enki became Ea: "...about 2500 B.C., Akkadians introduced the name Ea for Enki." (p. 3. Samuel Noah Kramer & John Maier. *Myths of Enki the Crafty God.* New York. Oxford University Press. 1989.) Abraham according to the biblical chronology compiled by some scholars was born circa 2100 B.C., and lived at Ur of the Chaldees (modern Tell al Muqayyar in Sumer according to some.)

Anderson on Yahweh's different name forms found in the Hebrew Bible: "It is not certain, however, that 'yahweh' was the oldest form of the name. A short form 'yah' appears 25 times in the Old Testament (Ex 15:2; and cultic cry 'hallelu-yah'= 'praise yah'). Sometimes the short form appears as 'yahu' or 'yo' as in proper names like Joel ('Yo is God') or Isaiah ('Yah is salvation')." (p. 409. vol. 2. B. W. Anderson. "God, Names of." pp. 407-416. George Arthur Buttrick. Editor. The Interpreter's Dictionary of the Bible. Nashville. Abingdon Press. 1962.)

Diane Wolkstein, in collaboration with the late Sumerologist Professor Samuel Noah Kramer noted that Enki possessed the secret to restoring the dead in the underworld back to life and a resurrection to the earth's surface. In the myth of Ishtar or Inanna's descent into the underworld, she tells her servant that if after three days and nights she does not return, he is to notify Enki who will effect her release (cf. pp.54, 61. Diane Wolkstein & Samuel Noah Kramer. Inanna, Queen of Heaven and Earth, Her Stories and Hymns From Sumer. New York Harper & Row, Publishers. 1983. ISBN 0-06-090854-8 pbk)

No progress has been made in locating the Israelite encampments, in identifying their route, or in fixing the site of Mount Sinai." (p. 28, Aviram Perevolotsky and Israel Finkelstein. "The Southern Sinai Exodus Route in Ecological Perspective." pp. 27-41. Biblical Archaeology Review. July/August. 1985. Vol. XI No. 4)

Repeated excavations and surveys throughout the entire area have not provided even the slightest evidence for activity in the late Bronze Age, not even a single sherd left by a tiny fleeing band of frightened refugees." (pp. 62-63, "Did the Exodus Happen?" Israel Finkelstein & Neil Asher Silberman. The Bible Unearthed, Archaeology's New Vision of Ancient Israel and the Origin of Its Sacred Texts. New York. The Free Press. 2001.)

Israelite version of a monolatry focused on Yahwe, but it still needs to be recognized that the worship of Yahwe persisted in areas of the Near East outside of Israel." (pp. 250-251. "From Israel's Largest Empire to the Fall of Samaria." Cyrus H. Gordon & Gary A. Rendsburg. The Bible and the Ancient Near East. New York & London. W. W. Norton & Company. 1997. [4th edition, 1965, 1958, 1953.])

Mari archives on the Euphrates give names of Amorites that some scholars have suggested are Yahweh names: Yawidim (Addu), Yawian, Yawiila, Yawium, Yawid, and Yawiya (p. 39.)"List of Amorite Personal Names." Herbert B. Huffmon. Amorite Personal Names in the Mari Texts: A Structural and Lexical Study. Baltimore, Maryland: The Johns Hopkins Press. 1965).

Finet comments, "the god Yawi is a newcomer, a syncretistic deity to whom his devotees claim to assimilate the local gods such as Ila/El or Adad or Dagan." Yawi, of course, is the same as Yahweh." (p. 284. Herbert B. Huffmon. "Yahweh and Mari." pp. 283-289, in Hans Goedicke. Editor. Near Eastern Studies in Honor of William Foxwell Albright. Baltimore, Maryland. The Johns Hopkins Press. 1971.)

There is no denying that the name Yahweh might have arisen otherwise, but it is worth while to bear in mind that so far as names are concerned, an element such as yahweh is best known in Amorite personal names and, in so far as early Canaanite is concerned, examples are restricted to a place name in Egyptian topographical lists and to a learned lexicographical text from Ugarit."
(p. 289.Herbert B. Huffmon. "Yahweh and Mari." pp. 283-289, in Hans Goedicke. Editor. Near Eastern Studies in Honor of William Foxwell Albright. Baltimore, Maryland. The Johns Hopkins Press. 1971.)

*** *** ***

Recent Books by Maximillien de Lafayette

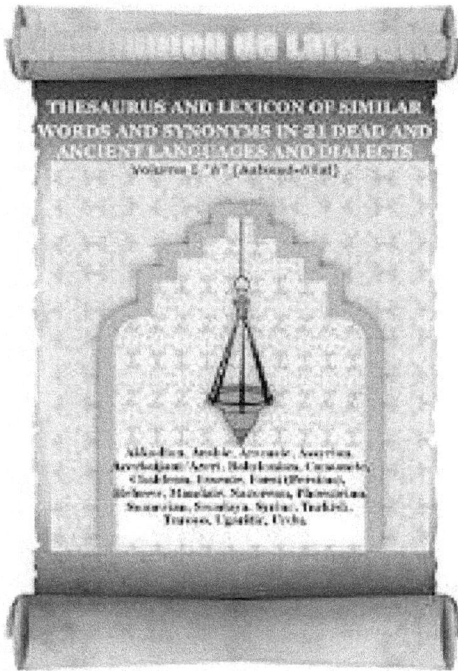

THESAURUS AND LEXICON OF SIMILAR WORDS AND SYNONYMS IN 21 DEAD AND ANCIENT LANGUAGES AND DIALECTS

A set of 20 volumes. THESAURUS & LEXICON OF SIMILAR WORDS & SYNONYMS IN 21 DEAD & ANCIENT LANGUAGES AND DIALECTS.

Akkadian, Arabic, Aramaic, Assyrian, Azerbaijani/Azeri, Babylonian, Canaanite, Chaldean, Essenic, Farsi (Persian), Hebrew, Mandaic, Nazorean, Phoenician, Sumerian, Swadaya, Syriac, Turkish, Turoyo, Ugaritic, Urdu.

The world's 1st dictionary/thesaurus/lexicon of its kind! A gem. A literary treasure! Written by the world's most prolific linguist who authored 21 dictionaries of dead and ancient languages known to mankind. Published by Times Square Press NY.

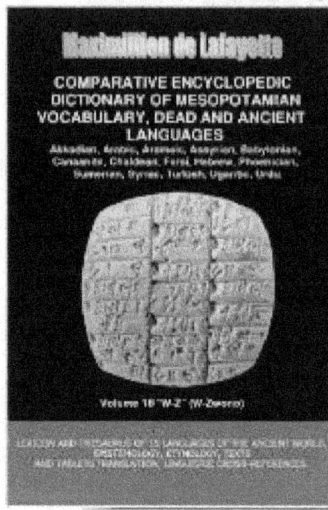

Comparative Encyclopedic Dictionary of Mesopotamian Vocabulary, Dead and Ancient Languages. Lexicon and Thesaurus of 15 Languages and Dialects of the Ancient World
A set of 18 volumes (Approximately 4,200 pages).

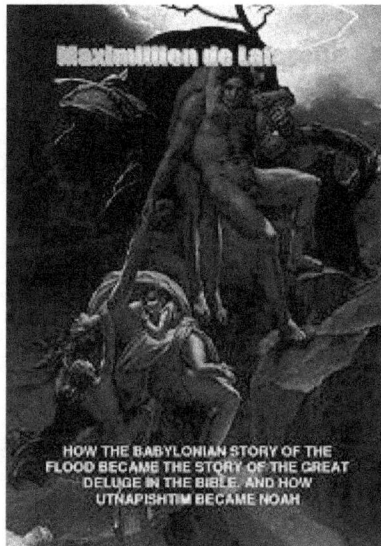

How the Babylonian Story of the Flood Became the Story of the Great Deluge in the Bible. And How Utnapishtim Became Noah.

From the content:
• Biblical stories taken from much older religions.
• The Babylonian Story of the Flood Versus the Biblical Story of the Flood.
• There is a difference of approximately 600 years between the Babylonian flood and the Biblical flood.
• Excerpts from the Mesopotamian texts, word-for-word, and my translation.
• Same stories in the Babylonian texts and the Bible:
• 1.The Anunnaki god Ea warned Utnapishtim about a flood.
• Instructions on how to build the boat.
• 2.Bringing animals to the boat.
• 3.The dove.
• 4.The birds are set free.
• 5.The boat resting on the top of a mountain.
• 6.Destroying mankind.
• 7.Reason for sending the flood.
• 8.Never again to bring a flood to earth and destroy

mankind.
- 9.The 7th day of the flood.
- 10. Seven days of flood: In the Bible.
- 11.Waiting for the 7th day.
- 12.Sealing the door and cover of the boat with pitch.
- 13.Making a roof (Cover for the boat).
- 14.The covenant.
- 15.Offerings and sacrifices.
- 16.The blessing of Utnapishtim and Noah.
- Characteristics and dissimilarities of the three Babylonian versions of the story of the flood, the Epic of Gilgamesh and Berossus' account.
- The Sumerian story of the flood according to Berossus, a priest of the cult of Marduk in Babylon.

Published by

TIMES SQUARE PRESS, NEW YORK
www.timessquarepress.com

Printed in the
United States of America
July 23, 2014

www.ingramcontent.com/pod-product-compliance
Lightning Source LLC
Chambersburg PA
CBHW020526030426
42337CB00011B/556